STEAM'S LAMENT

London Midland Engine Sheds
Volume I - 1A to 7D

Kevin Derrick

Strathwood

STEAM'S LAMENT

London Midland Engine Sheds
Volume I - 1A to 7D

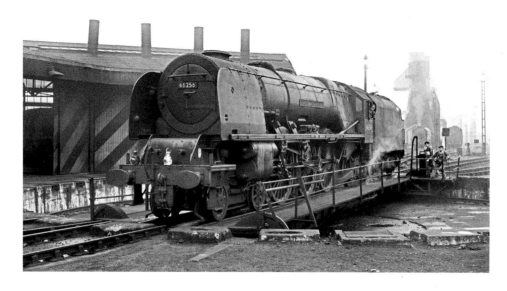

First published 2019
ISBN 978-1-905276-96-7

Copyright Strathwood Publishing 2019
Published by Strathwood Publishing, 9 Boswell Crescent, Inverness, IV2 3ET
Telephone 01463 234004
Printed by Akcent Media, Ltd.
www.strathwood.co.uk

Contents

This volume is compiled on the basis of the shed codes of 1948-1950 wherever possible

Opposite: A well turned out 46240 City of Coventry stands proudly at the head of the lines at 1A Willesden in March 1964, her home shed at this time. She was re-allocated to 5A Crewe North five months later in August and promptly withdrawn the following month. Just a year after this scene was taken at Willesden this fine locomotive was cut up by Cashmores in Great Bridge. *Strathwood Library Collection*

From the lack of locomotives on show this society visit during April 1962 cannot have taken place on a Sunday! However, a reasonably clean Britannia Pacific can be seen on shed, Willesden's allocation of steam locomotives remained fairly constant at around 130 to 140 through the 1950s but was reducing fast now in the early 1960s as diesel traction started to appear in greater numbers. *John Day Collection/Rail Photoprints*

Opposite: This 1922 built Armstrong Whitworth Class 4F has arrived from 15A Wellingborough during 1959 and stands alongside the shed's open store for all of those larger items that didn't require locking away. Also of note is that 43977 is one of those class members fitted with outside steam pipes. *Strathwood Library Collection*

Today is obviously washout day for this collection of Willesden's Standard Class 2MT Moguls on 8 August 1965. There were eleven of these versatile locomotives allocated here during this year, although the shed closed to steam on 27 September soon after this shot was taken. *R C Riley/The Transport Treasury*

Opposite: Standards of cleanliness have certainly slipped for this Jinty Class 3F, 47432 which had come to Willesden in December 1964 when nearby Cricklewood had closed to steam. Here on 17 January 1965, she finds temporary sanctuary until being withdrawn from 1A in August of this year. *Late Hugh Ballantyne/ Rail Photoprints*

Another glorious red Duchess is seen by the coaler at Willesden during 1964 with a fine head of steam in her boiler as her crew make their way off shed. It is difficult to see how the shed staff could have loaded any more spent ash into the 16ton mineral wagon to the left of the Pacific. *Strathwood Library Collection*

Opposite: Both the shed pilot 47501 and some of the coaler and ash plant staff catch a breather at Willesden on 21 May 1964. This Jinty had been a London engine throughout the British Railway's era, firstly at 1D Devons Road in Bow before arriving here at 1A during December 1957, withdrawal came in August 1964. *Nigel Kendall/Anistr.com*

The rumble and dust cloud have subsided around this visiting Stanier Class 8F, 48474 as her crew have wisely taken leave of the footplate, for now, most likely replenishing their tea cans with boiling water to see them through the duty ahead. ***Strathwood Library Collection***

One of the driver's duties before heading off shed was the time-honoured ritual of oiling around all of the locomotive's lubrication points as here on this Fairburn Class 4MT 42120 from 1C Watford. Willesden was also hosting one of the Ivatt pioneer diesels too on 11 May 1950. *Colour Rail*

Opposite: The fireman walks alongside 46240 City of Coventry as they head down the yard at Willesden on 18 August 1963, although she is looking a little less well cared for than in our previous view taken in her last year of traffic. *Frank Hornby*

We take our leave of Willesden on Sunday 8 October 1961 with this party inside the roundhouse to record one of the two rebuilt Jubilees 45735 Comet. *David T. Williams*

The newer forms of traction already outnumber steam in this splendid view of 1B Camden on 10 August 1962. *Rail Photoprints*

Opposite: The raised metal numerals unique to 45552 Silver Jubilee stand proudly on the cab side of this now sadly neglected once "royal" engine as her crew take water prior to turning at 1B Camden in 1962. When originally built by the LMS as 5552 Silver Jubilee was the first of her class in June 1934 from Crewe Works. However, 5552 swapped identities with classmate 5642 in April 1935, as part of this 5552 was also given a special livery of all over black (it originally had been, like the rest of the class, painted crimson lake) with silver lining and specially cast chrome numbers and named as Silver Jubilee to mark the silver jubilee of King George V. This distinctive colour scheme was retained until the 1948 nationalization of British Railways. The rest of its class were thereafter officially known as the Jubilee Class. It originally had a low degree superheat domeless boiler but received a high degree superheat domed boiler in 1940. The loco was allocated to several London Midland Region sheds during its British Railway's service days, including Longsight, Crewe North, Carlisle Upperby, Bushbury, and Edge Hill. It was renumbered 45552 in September 1951, receiving the new cast numbers seen here. It was also given a livery of Brunswick green at the same time, although in this view it is well obscured by a generous layer of soot and dirt. The end of this fine locomotive's reign would come upon withdrawal in September 1964, being scrapped by Cashmores, of Great Bridge in April 1965.
Rail Photoprints Collection

A visit to the former London & North Western Railway shed here at Camden on 3 April 1957 finds long term resident to 1B, 46247 City of Liverpool stabled along the side of shed building. The Ulster Express headboard was for a service connecting Euston with Heysham and the ferry service across the Irish Sea to Belfast.
Tony Butcher

The original roundhouse for servicing locomotives here at Camden stands in the background to Jinty tank 47529 on 16 February 1958. This original roundhouse had ceased to be used for servicing before World War Two, it was given listed status in 1954 and opened as a theatre ten years later.
Richard C. Riley/The Transport Treasury

Opposite: The days for big Pacifics at Camden are drawing to a close here around 1963 as the fireman trims his coal on this Britannia, he will soon be riding as a second man most likely on board English Electric Type 4s before they, in turn, give way to AC electric locomotives.
John Day Collection/Rail Photoprints

Opposite: In the early summer of 1960, Royal Scot 46156 The South Wales Borderer awaits the signal to move off the shed at Camden and drop down the bank to Euston. Shame on the fireman for going out on the road without sweeping off the ash from below the smokebox. *John Day Collection/Rail Photoprints*

When seen being turned on Camden's turntable on 20 September 1958, the rather clean 46101 Royal Scots Grey was allocated to 5A Crewe North, in June the following year it would find itself re-allocated here to 1B Camden. *R.C. Riley/The Transport Treasury*

Opposite: A return journey towards Manchester is likely next for 9A Longsight allocated 70032 Tennyson, whereas 1B Camden's 46229 Duchess of Hamilton is destined for a more prestigious duty it seems here during 1959. *John Day Collection/Rail Photoprints*

On 28 April 1962, 46245 City of London undergoes a boiler washout inside the long shed at Camden before return to duty among the increasing numbers of invading diesels. Things look a little tidier in here undercover and closer to the shed foreman's offices. *Rail Online*

A smartly turned out 46207 Princess Arthur of Connaught is being shuffled around the yard of its home shed around 1960 as an English Electric Type 1 lurks in the background. The shed here closed to steam on 9 September 1963 and then completely as of 3 January 1966.
The Transport Treasury

The London & North Western Railway originally established an engine shed here at Watford which became coded 1C as a sub-shed in LMS days to Willesden. On 7 May 1960, home allocated Fowler Class 4F 44440 is kept outside by some of the Class 4MT tanks still employed on local services. The far side of the shed building had originally been built in the same style as the near side before being repaired during the thirties. Access for spotters couldn't have been easier if you were prepared to cross the slow lines and stroll into the shed yard.

Late Norman Browne/Strathwood Library Collection

On a bright but cold day in December 1962, a well turned out Fairburn Class 4MT 42096 sizzles nicely in the shed yard here at Watford. Although Sulzer Type 2 diesels took over most of their duties in the areas around this time, remarkably this tank locomotive hung on here until the shed closed to steam on 29 March 1965. The shed buildings were used as a diesel stabling point for a short while after closure before they were demolished and the area being re-used as a station car park.
Win Wall/Strathwood Library Collection

Also on shed that same sunny winter's day was Black Five 45048 from 5B Crewe South along with Ivatt Class 2MT 46423 on its home shed. The steam shed at Watford lay in between the mainline and the route to St. Albans the platform for the branch can be seen behind the Black Five's tender. *Win Wall/Strathwood Library Collection*

Above: As a result of the proximity to Watford Junction station the shed yard was fairly compact with access being afforded from both routes. We cannot be sure that the large lumps of coal onboard Fowler Class 4F 44340 are soundly stacked and not likely to fall off in this view of some shunting at 1C Watford. *The Transport Treasury*

Left: The coal stage here at Watford was tucked away behind the shed building, thus meaning spotters would have to be observant if they were to get the numbers of the likes of this Ivatt Class 4MT 43018 stabled here on 8 March 1964, if they were passing by on the mainline non-stop. *Colour Rail*

The east end of London was heavily bombed during World War Two and the former North London Railway's locomotive shed at Devons Road in Bow was still showing signs of the blitz ten years later as the rebuilding work was taking place in the area. One of the uglier double chimney fitted Ivatt Class 4MT stands in the yard on 16 April 1955, this was the home shed for 43001 at this time. *Rail Online*

Devons Road coded 1D was the home to almost forty of these Jinty Class 3Fs, such as 47482 seen on 23 March 1957. Until the arrival of the diesels in the late 1950s when a short-lived conversion of the old steam shed was given over to an influx of Type 1s and diesel shunters brought in to comply with the London Clean Air Act, A small number of the surviving North London Railway Class 2F 0-6-0Ts could still be found here such as 58857, which was the last one in the area, when withdrawn in April 1958. The converted diesel shed stands in the background, this opened in August 1958 and closed on 10 February 1964, however steam had ceased here as of 9 September 1963. *Rail Online & Strathwood Library Collection*

Opposite: Rugby's importance during the steam era came about as a result of the town was a convenient point to conduct engine changes and its proximity as an important junction location. Concequently, two large sheds were built with a fitting shop between them employing nearly 900 men at its peak. Thereby Rugby became the main shed to six sub-sheds in the area including Warwick, Coventry, Peterborough, Stamford, Seaton and Market Harborough. The size of the shed complex also made it suitable for the storage of locomotives during any lulls in traffic the winter months. In this scene from the late 1950s, two of the early diesel shunters provide a backdrop to one of Bescot's Class G2As and a Black Five awaiting repairs. Rugby was coded as 2A until 9 September 1963 when it became 1F, it closed to steam as of 24 May 1965 and completely on 31 December 1968.
Strathwood Library Collection

Among those locomotives held in storage over the winter months of 1959 and into 1960 was this Class 4P Compound 41162 tucked away alongside its home shed of Rugby on 16 April 1960. In fact, it was reported as being in store here since October 1957, a long-awaited return to service would not be forthcoming as it was withdrawn officially a few weeks later in June before heading to Gorton Works for disposal in August the same year.
Strathwood Library Collection

A quick last minute check by the driver of Class G2A 49448 from 5B Crewe South before heading back northwards on 1 February 1963 once again from Rugby, having been fitted with a snow plough during the Great Freeze. *Rail Online*

There would be no redemption for Stanier Class 2P 41909 held in storage with a classmate alongside the shed at Rugby on 20 September 1959. It had been a Watford engine at nationalisation, passing to 2C Warwick in August 1955 before arriving here at Rugby in November 1958, its final withdrawal came in November 1959. ***Strathwood Library Collection***

Safely nestled away inside at Rugby on 24 April 1965 was Fairburn Class 4MT 42103 wearing its 1G Woodford Halse shed plate it was destined never to work again and would head to Newport to be scrapped at the hands of Buttigiegs. ***George Woods***

Left: At the time of nationalisation, Nuneaton was coded 2D, it took over the code of 2B from Bletchley on 8 July 1950. This was the scene here at Nuneaton as 2B on 2 September 1961. *Strathwood Library Collection*

Below: Still showing signs of the changes of the time outside Nuneaton shed on 12 June 1949 was Class G2A 49268 on its home territory at this time. *Strathwood Library Collection*

This was a very busy shed located in between the Coventry route and the WCML, the arrival of the electrification masts in the background to this view of 47653 as the Nuneaton shed pilot on 7 October 1962, suggest the writing is already on the wall for the shed's future. It would soon be re-coded once again as a sub-shed to Crewe as 5E on 9 September the following year. *Rail Online*

No cast shed plates for these two Black Fives 45001 and 45065 inside at 5E Nuneaton on 20 June 1965. In the 1950s it had an allocation of over seventy locomotives, by this stage, it was down to half that number. Finally, the shed lost all steam in March 1966 and closed completely on 6 June the same year. *George Woods*

Northampton shed would be another to ring in the changes as far as its shed codes would go, starting out in the British Railway's era as 2C until 8 July 1950 when it became 4B as Warwick shed then took over as 2C. Staying as 4B until 2 March 1952, Northampton then took up cast shed plates for its allocation as 2E, which would last until 9 September 1963.

The final shed code for Northampton shed would then be as 1H until it closed completely on 27 September 1965. Wearing its correct shed code as 2E this push and pull fitted Ivatt Class 2MT simmers outside the running shed at Northampton on 30 July 1963. *Rail Photoprints*

A return visit here five days later finds the now withdrawn 41218 the other push and pull fitted Ivatt Class 2MT dumped at the Duston Junction West end of the shed yard, ready to be hauled away for scrap to Cashmores at Great Bridge. *John Evans*

Smoking away on 17 August 1965 at Northampton shed is Jinty 47590 on shed pilot duties when the shed closed the following month this plucky little survivor found more work firstly at 5B Crewe South and then at 5D Stoke. *John Evans*

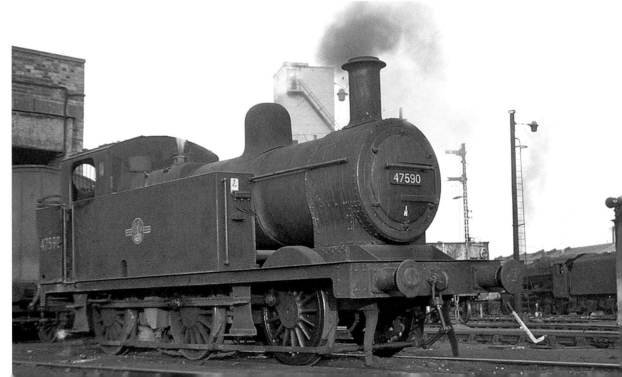

A return to happier days for Northampton shed coded as 2E on 5 September 1954, as it hosts Fowler Patriot Class 45504 Royal Signals from Crewe North sandwiched between several eight coupled designs on this Sunday visit. Northampton also retained a sub-shed at Blisworth from July 1950 until December 1962. *Eric Sawford/The Transport Treasury*

Coventry shed was coded as 2F until 8 July 1950 when it became 2D, this was the scene on 13 February 1955, the shed closed completely on 17 November 1958. Another ex-LNWR shed within the area was at Warwick which was coded as 2C when visited on 13 September 1957, it would close on 1 February the following year. *Both: Strathwood Library Collection*

Our final sub-shed to Rugby that remains for us to visit was here at Market Harborough coded as 2F from 8 October 1955 until 20 April 1958 when it became 15F as a sub-shed to Leicester Midland. Of interest in the background to this view, we can see the stored gas turbine locomotive 18000 which was kept here from October 1964 until early 1965. *Strathwood Library Collection*

An earlier visit in 1962 found Fowler Class 4F 44530 unable to squeeze into the small two road engine shed at this cramped location which would close completely in 1965. *Rail Online*

A selection of Ivatt Moguls welcome us to Bescot in April 1963, it had been coded as 3A from nationalisation until 20 June 1960 when it took up 21B as its new code. *Colour Rail*

There was much for the visitor to see here at Bescot on Sunday 26 March 1961. *Colour Rail*

As an important shed within the Walsall area of Birmingham, visits to Bescot could always be relied upon to provide a wealth of freight locomotives, with Stanier Mogul 42977 prominent in this 1958 scene. *Rail Online*

There are a number of engines for the Bescot shed staff to keep an eye upon as they are slowly brought back up to the boil on Sunday 23 April 1961 ready for duty once more. *David T. Williams*

Although nearby Bushbury coded 3B enjoyed an allocation of Jubilees it was also home to a few more of Johnson's Class 2F 0-6-0s such as 58124, found alongside the shed on 10 June 1961. It was also now coded as 21C from 1960 until 1963 when it became 2K until final closure on 12 April 1965. Bushbury shed enjoyed a stay of execution as it was to have closed on 7 April 1964, the wooden gallows above 58124 were to help train staff about the pending 25kv electrification wiring clearances. *Colour Rail*

Another of these ex-Midland Railway, Johnson Class 2Fs was found taking shelter within its home shed of 3C Walsall Rycroft on 29 December 1957. Coded as 3C, the shed was closed to steam in June 1958 and given over to DMUs. It retained the same shed code until 20 June 1960 when it adopted the code 21F until 9 September 1963 when it then took up 2G until closure in April 1967. *Colour Rail*

In comparison to the black country sheds a touch of glamour in green with an ex-works Jubilee, 45595 Southern Rhodesia in the shed yard at Aston which had been coded 3D but was now 21D when this view was taken on 29 July 1962. Having just visited the coaler Black Five 44872 was now on the turntable here at Aston in August 1963.
Strathwood Library Collection & Colour Rail

Opposite: Also on shed at Aston in 1963 was this Hughes Crab with 10C Fleetwood painted on the smokebox door. *Rail Online*

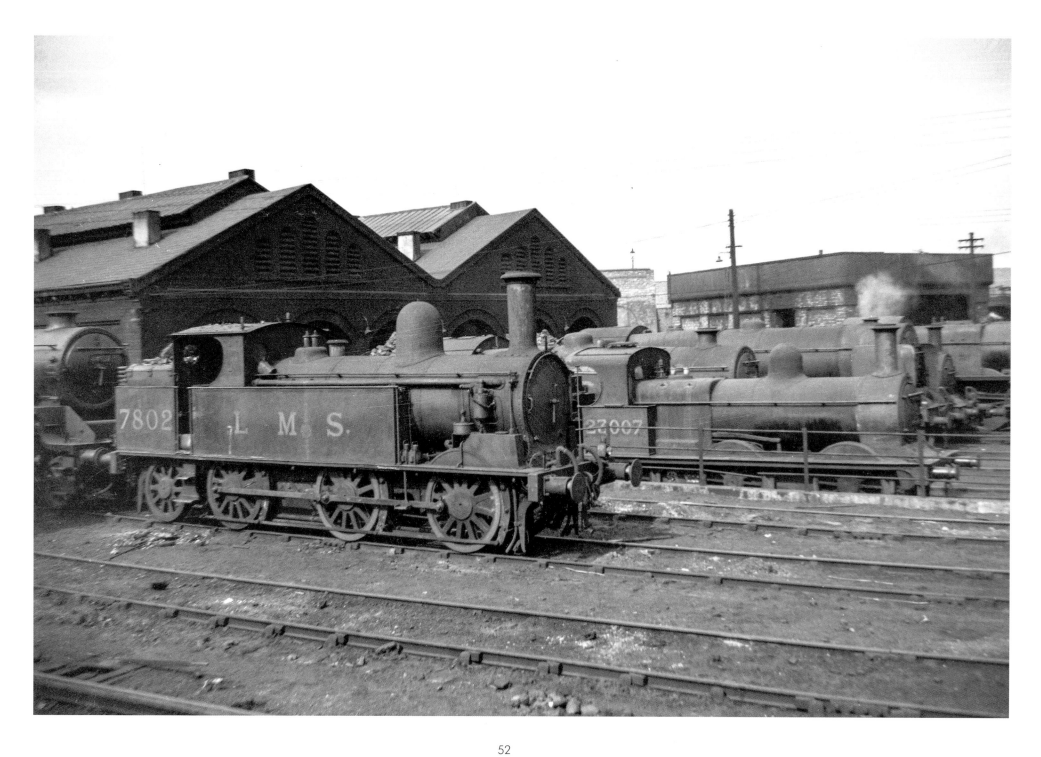

At least something had been done to this Fowler Compound 41166 from Longsight which was seen in the shed yard at Monument Lane on 3 July 1948, as a start towards the new liveries.
Strathwood Library Collection

Monument Lane stables this home allocated Fowler Compound in the mid-fifties. It once had two sub-sheds at Albion and Tipton to its name. Code changes in 1960 saw it become 21E before taking up 2H on 9 September 1963, although steam had ceased here 12 February 1962. Final closure for Monument Lane was listed as new year's day 1967.
Strathwood Library Collection

Opposite: The decline of 3E Monument Lane started soon after World War Two as express turns were focused upon Bushbury. A visit on 27 March 1949 hardly suggest nationalisation had taken place at all.
The Transport Treasury

In 1948, Bletchley shed was coded as 2B, but in 1950 as part of a huge re-coding exercise throughout British Railways, it became 4A, although it would only retain this new shed code until 2 March 1952 when it was tagged on as 1E as part of the London Division. Bletchley shed also enjoyed a number of sub-sheds such as Aylesbury, Cambridge, Leighton Buzzard, Newport Pagnell and Oxford (LMR). Having just taken coal from the mechanical grab, Jubilee 45660 Rooke moves off once again on Sunday 14 July 1963. *David T. Williams*

The grab is in action again on 7 February 1964 for Hughes Crab 42783, with Standard Class 2MT 84002 next in the line for coal at Bletchley. *Colour Rail*

The shed roof at Bletchley was renewed during 1954, which as can be seen improved the working conditions for the shed staff considerably. This is Royal Scot 46146 The Rifle Brigade having its motion attended to and repaired a year later before the glass above became really sooty once again. *Strathwood Library Collection*

It was easy to get the numbers of anything on one of Bletchley's many sub-sheds here at Aylesbury, with 1G Woodford Halse's, Fairburn Class 4MT 42250 in residence on 22 May 1964, which would be its last year in service. Officially the shed here at Aylesbury had already closed completely on 18 June 1962. *The Transport Treasury*

A great chance to play spot the difference here at Leighton Buzzard another of Bletchley's sub-sheds. Firstly on 27 February 1955, with Class G2 49450 now allocated to 9D Buxton but previously a Bletchley engine, had they kidnapped it back? Then opposite, with another view taken here on 3 June 1962 with 49287 and 49106 being identified. This was after the shed had been cut back and re-roofed a couple of years earlier. These repairs would not save it as it would close later this year on 5 November with resultant light engine movements back and forth to Bletchley taking place as a result. *Both: Strathwood Library Collection*

Harking back to the pre-grouping era the LNWR served the city of Oxford, but as the GWR refused access to their engine shed facilities it required a separate shed to be constructed at Rewley Road opposite the GWR shed. With a nationalised railway it was soon obvious of the savings to be made by servicing locomotives off the London Midland Region across at the Western Region's shed 81F. As a result, the shed seen here in 1949 became disused after 3 December 1950, although the structure remained standing for a while afterwards. *Strathwood Library Collection*

A rudimentary wooden shed was provided within Wolverton Works for servicing the four Special DX tanks which remained in use until the late 1950s as we see here on 19 March 1955.
Strathwood Library Collection

Five of these Class 2F Special Tanks passed into British Railway's stock in 1948, one found use until December 1950 within Crewe Works, with four of them complete with their cast cab side numberplates shunting withing Wolverton Carriage Works. Three of them are gathered here alongside somewhat primitive shed facilities during a lunch break within the works during the 1950s. *Strathwood Library Collection*

Crewe has always held an important place in the hearts of just about every British railway enthusiast. With views such as this one from the top of the coaling and ash plant facilities looking across to the station and Crewe North engine shed coded 5A we can easily see why. This view was most likely taken around 1961 as the electrification masts have been installed. Our photographer was, of course, a much-respected footplate cameraman with easier access than those who did not work upon the railway. *Late Jim Carter/Rail Online*

Another shot from around 1960-61 of the then everyday scenes, with the likes of this one hundred and four tons of Stanier Princess Royal Pacific in the shape of 46209 Princess Beatrice being turned and made ready for duty on its home shed. With deliveries of English Electric Type 4 diesels happening every month, this was a sight that would not last for much longer. *Late Jim Carter/Rail Online*

Just back into service and sparkling in the sunshine around 1960-61 this ex-works Ivatt Class 2MT Mogul will most likely be put onto a duty by the Crewe North shed foreman to get the locomotive back towards its home shed of 21B Bescot. *Late Jim Carter/Rail Online*

What finer sight to behold from the 1960s at Crewe North with a background of the newer semi-roundhouse shed building from the mid-1950s, as Stanier's Coronation Pacific 46256 Sir William A.Stanier F.R.S. stands on the turntable here at 5A on 21 July 1964, The locomotive was withdrawn from service just a few months later in October 1964.
Paul Claxton/Rail Photoprints Collection

An ex-works Class 9F and Royal Scot 46170 British Legion have just been tripped across from Crewe Works here to 5A to take up service once again. This particular Royal Scot was always bulled up every November as part of marking Remembrance Day. *Late Jim Carter/Rail Online*

Opposite: Another view taken by the 70' turntable allowing access to the newer semi-roundhouse built in 1953, with one of the forty, Stanier designed Class 5MT Moguls about to be parked up just where our photographer is standing on 25 June 1960. *Colour Rail*

An earlier view from a similar location of Royal Scot 46138 The London Irish Rifleman during the early 1950s provides a backdrop showing the soon to be demolished No.2 and No. 3 engine sheds known as the Abba or Abbabyssinia and The Cage respectively. *Rail Online*

Opposite: A view looking out from the new semi-roundhouse in the early 1960s to appreciate the elegance of an ex-works Brunswick Green Jubilee, as 45565 Victoria from 55A Leeds Holbeck awaits her chance to head back across the Pennines to her home shed once more.
Late Jim Carter/Rail Online

The rundown remains of the Abyssinia and The Cage can be glimpsed in the background to 46169 The Boy Scout as the Royal Scot is carefully balanced onto the turntable at Crewe North on 18 August 1962. A quiet moment in The Cage in the early 1960s affords a chance for a young footplateman to pose from the cab window of Duchess 46254 City of Stoke-on-Trent.

Photos: Colour Rail & Late Jim Carter/Rail Online

The majesty and importance of Stanier's Duchesses were exemplified by those in their distinctive lined maroon liveries such as 46240 City of Coventry under the coaler. Even the addition of the warning stripe to 46245 City of London to warn that it should not pass south from here at Crewe under the electric catenary does little to detract when it was photographed on 1 September 1964. *Both: Late Jim Carter/Rail Photoprints*

As the 1950s drew to a close 5A Crewe had 125 steam locomotives among its allocation of which at least half of them were named. Add to this visiting engines such as this Rebuilt Patriot 45523 Bangor on 25 June 1960, also visits to 5B Crewe South with almost as many engines again, not to forget the locomotive works and Gresty Lane shed and we can see why Crewe was such a mecca for spotters. Here an ex-works Austerity has been released from the nearby locomotive works at Crewe around 1950 at a time when the new lion and wheel emblem was just about to be used, hence the blank tender. *Photos: Colour Rail & Rail Online*

Although 5A Crewe North closed on 24 May 1965, the code of 5A was given to Crewe Diesel Depot which opened the same day. Meanwhile, Crewe South coded 5B carried on servicing what remained of the steam fleet arriving here. The flavour of steam locomotives to be found here at Crewe South tended to be more mixed traffic and freight designs. Although visitors such as the Hall from the Western Region on the right-hand side in the view opposite were often found as here on 8 April 1962, after the closure of Gresty Lane shed. The lighting gantries dominate in the two views of both ends of the shed.
Photos: Strathwood Library Collection & Rail Online

As late as 1959 the now rundown running shed at Crewe South was cut back and re-roofed by British Railways. Opposite, this is how things looked on 29 October 1967 a week before the shed closed to steam, whereas we can gauge from this view dating from 1952 that the rebuilding was well overdue at the start of the 1950s. However, in austerity Britain such opportunities to set men to work and improve working conditions were often delayed by available funds and politics, some things never change! Even with the nearby Crewe Diesel Depot being opened in 1965, a large number of diesels were to be seen stabled here at Crewe South up until the shed's total closure. **Photos: Strathwood Library & Rail Online**

Sadly the once clean, lined green Britannias complete with their nameplates were looking rather unkempt by the time these spotters made their way around the lines at Crewe South on 19 February 1967. Steam was now very much in decline with most of the shed's steam turns being freight as they had been a decade beforehand, this ensured that Crewe South did not close at the same time as Crewe North in 1965, at the opening of the large new diesel depot. We should not also forget that Crewe also had a new electric depot opened in the early 1960s too.

Colin Rodgers/Strathwood Library Collection

The last real everyday glamour to be seen at Crewe South was perhaps here in 1964 with a visit of 46256 Sir William A.Stanier FRS.
Strathwood Library Collection

Opposite & this page: This Ivatt Mogul has already been seen on page 29 at Devons Road, Bow in an earlier guise with a double-chimney, aside from now having a single chimney it has also been paired up with a tender complete with a tablet recess as it stands withdrawn at Crewe South in September 1967. The next move will soon be to Ward's at Killamarsh where it was scrapped in December the same year. All opportunities had to be taken at this time to record steam while it was still here such as on a cold and bright 2 February again during that last year here in 1967. *Photos: Strathwood Library Collection & Jerry Beddows*

Opposite: No point firing up the Drewry diesel shunter to move it around Crewe South as there was still plenty of steam available on 22 August 1959, such as Stanier Class 5MT Mogul 42979 from 3D Aston. *Colour Rail*

As with Wolverton Works, there was also a servicing shed within Crewe Works albeit a more modern brick-built facility. This was the line-up outside the shed in September 1964 before the diesels took over. *Rail Photoprints*

Opposite & this page: The electrification masts signal the demise for 5C Stafford shed in both of these views, even though it was easily seen from the station its proximity to Crewe has perhaps led to it being under photographed. Making a fuss as it moves off shed on 18 August 1962 was Standard Class 5MT 73025, whilst a Stanier Class 4MT takes both coal and water. A second appearance for Royal Scot 46170 British Legion this time standing outside the shed at Stafford on 6 May 1962, this would be her last year in service. *Photos: The Bluebell Railway Museum & Rail Photoprints*

Just how close the station and the shed were at Stafford shows well here as Johnson/Fowler Class 2P 40332 from 5A Crewe North has been sent here to 5C Stafford for storage to get it out of the way during the winter months at its home shed during the early 1950s. *Rail Online*

Opposite: With a backdrop of the Stafford coaler Royal Scot 46148 The Manchester Regiment makes an impressive sight having arrived most likely with a running in turn from Crewe earlier in the day. The shed closed to steam and became a diesel stabling point after 19 July 1965. *Colour Rail*

All of the engine sheds looked at so far were established by the London & North Western Railway, here at Stoke-on-Trent it was within the domain of the North Staffordshire Railway. The shed code right through the British Railway's era remained as 5D. As with many engine sheds, it would be the ferro-concrete coaling plant that would dominate the scene, this view was taken in 1966 of the straight shed. Steam activity here officially ceased as of 7 August 1967. **Strathwood Library Collection**

Opposite: This undated shot within the once impressive original roundhouse at 5D Stoke-on-Trent is thought to have been taken in 1954, when local side Port Vale F.C. played West Bromwich Albion in the semi-final of the F.A. Cup at Villa Park, with 42665 dressed up for the supporters special. The Stanier Class 4MT was based at 5F Uttoxeter at this time. **Colour Rail**

The somewhat cramped nature of the fan of tracks around 5D Stoke's straight shed is evident in this view. The possibility for accidents and collisions whilst shunting in the dark within the shed yard look extreme in this view from 1965. The distinctive ash disposal gantry here at Stoke can be seen to the left. ***Strathwood Library Collection***

The scarcely photographed former North Staffordshire Railway shed at Alsager coded 5E enjoyed an allocation of around eighteen locomotives when recorded here in 1955, it would close on 18 June 1962. *John Bell/The Transport Library*

Opposite: Another North Staffordshire Railway rarity it seems was 5F Uttoxeter although it lasted a little longer, closing on 7 December 1964. With only a small allocation of fewer than ten locomotives at any one time, it must be assumed 5F shed plates for collectors would be rare indeed. Indeed this duo on shed around 1960 both carry 5D Stoke-on-Trent shed plates. *Colour Rail*

A return to ex-LNWR territory next here at 6A Chester in 1955 with appropriately enough one of their Class G2A 0-8-0s, 49230 from 5B Crewe South as these two railwaymen discuss what's next. The allocation of locomotives at Chester increased from just under forty in 1950 to almost fifty by the end of the decade as British Railways standard designs ousted the shed's 4-4-0s. *Strathwood Library Collection*

Opposite: The engine shed here at Chester was rebuilt by the LMS after the war and further altered by British Railways in the late 1950s. Visiting during 1965 was Stanier Class 4MT 42606 from 8H Birkenhead. *Rail Online*

A more impressive visitor here at Chester for servicing was Willesden's Brittania 70034 Thomas Hardy which looks set to take over a North Wales express towards Euston. *Late Jim Carter/Rail Online*

The appearance of Austerity 2-8-0 90384 at Chester during 1964 suggests they would have been the very last locomotive that any engine cleaners would have been put to work on, not that there were any cleaners to be found by this date anyway. *Rail Photoprints*

A Sunday shed visit would always add more locomotives to any spotter's notebooks as here at Chester on 24 March 1957. The condition of Jinty 47297 conveys a recent works overhaul most likely to have been at either Derby or Horwich. *Rail Online*

Under the LMS, Mold Junction had been coded as 6B and this was not to change at all right through to closure on 18 April 1966. On 26 June 1964, 42765 one of Birkenhead's Hughes Crabs was among those on the shed. The thirteen Austerity 2-8-0s allocated here at the close of the fifties had given way to fifteen Stanier Class 8Fs by this time. **George Woods**

Right: Seen inside catching the sunshine just before closure Standard Class 4MT 75071 exhibits the lazy trend towards painting on locomotives shed codes crudely in place of the traditional cast shed plates. **Jim Winkley**

Opposite: We do not have to travel far to reach 6B Mold Junction shed as it is just three miles west of Chester. Although it was originally an ex-LNWR shed by the start of the sixties it was also servicing all of the Western Region's freight locomotives working into the district. Although by the time of this view around 1965, the area was dominated by ex-LMS, British Railways Standards and diesels. **Rail Online**

Things were much quieter on Wednesday 9 July 1958 for oiling round Stanier Class 4MT 42608 on its home shed. *Alec Swain/The Transport Treasury*

Right: The shed code for Birkenhead changed to 8H as of 9 September 1963 and continued with regular steam such as this Stanier Class 8F seen here during October 1966, until 6 November 1967. *Strathwood Library Collection*

Opposite: Recalling Western Region glories of the past, two enthusiast's specials were run to Birkenhead Woodside on 4 March 1967, this meant that 6C Birkenhead shed which had been an LNWR & GWR Joint Railway shed when built hosted the now preserved 7029 Clun Castle for servicing. *Tony Butcher*

There were forty-one ex-GWR locomotives based here at the start of the fifties, this had fallen to just two by the close of the decade. There were a number of tank locomotives some of which were equipped with bells for working in the nearby docks. This Class 0F 47006 was less than three years old when photographed among a selection of much older ex-GWR 2021 Class panniers at Birkenhead on 30 March 1956. In fact, this Standard Class 9F went into service just two months after 47006 seen opposite, both worked for approximately thirteen years due to the influx of diesels that followed them into service. When seen at Birkenhead on 27 September 1967, 92002 had a matter of weeks left to go before being withdrawn in November when the shed closed to steam.

Photos: Rail Online & Colour Rail

Opposite: The scrap road at Birkenhead awaits thinning out to scrap dealers when seen on 18 February 1967, meanwhile a party of enthusiasts are able to roam free-range around the yard on this cold and misty Saturday. In the background, several more Standard Class 9Fs are to be seen. When nearby 6F Bidston closed in early 1963, Birkenhead took over a number of iron-ore trains using Class 9Fs. By 1966, the allocation of the class here had swollen to over fifty locomotives. *Colour Rail*

The rundown of iron-ore workings coupled to the use of diesels saw a reduction in numbers for this once large fleet of Class 9Fs, among their number was this former Crosti boiler example showing the most basic of shed code identification as 8H, as Birkenhead's Mollington Street shed had now become by 1965. When steam finished on 6 November 1967 the extensive shed buildings were used to stable diesels until well into the following decade and provided a comfortable roost for hundreds of pigeons too. *Rail Online*

Opposite: A return to the city of Chester once again now to visit the former Cheshire Lines Committee shed 6D Chester Northgate where a frozen Robinson ROD 63686 from 39A Gorton sits out the snow storm on 19 January 1958. This Robert Stephenson & Co Ltd product from February 1918 would go on and see just over four years more service afterwards. *Colour Rail*

A push-pull fitted Ivatt Class 2MT wears a 6D Chester Northgate shed plate in this view which shows the local bus depot in the background on 30 August 1959. The shed was located to the east side of Northgate station. It closed to steam on 4 January 1960 and was used by diesel railcars for a while afterwards. *Strathwood Library Collection*

Another ROD visitor 63722 to Chester Northgate on 20 July 1952 with Class C13 67436 on its home shed. Another locomotive to wear a 6D shed plate was this Fowler Class 4MT 42417 on shed here by the coal stage on 16 May 1959. Only around ten locomotives were allocated here at any one time.
Photos: Rail Online & Strathwood Library Collection

The Ivatt Class 2MT is on home turf here at 6D Chester Northgate during 1956 whereas the former GCR Class N5 69335 has worked here from 6E Wrexham Rhosdhu. *Colour Rail*

Another ex-GCR locomotive is on hand to greet as we call into 6E Wrexham Rhosdhu shed during 1952. This Class C13 would be withdrawn a couple of years later as newer Ivatt Class 2MTs and Standard Class 3MTs arrived to replace the pre-grouping locomotives. The repairs to the shed roof appear to be more of a temporary nature as we see one of 6G Llandudno Junction's Ivatt Class 2MTs outside a few years later. The shed here moved to the Western Region as 84K on 1 February 1958 and closed on 4 January 1960, although it was used to store locomotives for a while afterwards. *Photos: The Transport Treasury & Rail Online*

Opposite: Another ex-GCR shed within this district was at Bidston coded 6F, the depot was just five-minutes walk towards the docklands near Birkenhead North station. As can be seen, it enjoyed a variety of locomotives both large and small. With 47166 tucked away at the rear on 7 April 1957, whereas another visit two years earlier on 19 July found 68034, 92047, 47674 and 64740 among its residents.
Photos: *Strathwood Library Collection & Rail Online*

Above: As we have already mentioned the nearby shed at Birkenhead Mollington Street took over the duties from 6F Bidston upon its closure on 11 February 1963. There would have been no indication of this when visited in the fifties with this duo of recently built Standard Class 9Fs 92045 and 92046 freshly allocated here in May 1956, joining 92047 which had already arrived here. ***Rail Online***

Although Llandudno Junction shed had been established by the LNWR most of the engines to be seen here by the mid-fifties were of Midland Railway heritage. These too would be swept aside as the ex-LNWR locomotives had before them when deliveries of Ivatt and Standard designs appeared. During much of the year, the shed yard was used to store spare or reserve locomotive stocks as here in 1956 with a rake of Midland Compounds. *Both: Strathwood Library Collection*

Opposite: A few years later and another line of stored locomotives have been sent here for winter hibernation. By the early sixties, it would be lines of stored Caprotti Black Fives and more Ivatt and Standard Class 2MTs instead. *The Transport Treasury*

Above: Originally coded as 7A by the LMS this code remained until 2 March 1952 when it became 6G. The shed's allocation of locomotives remained around thirty-five examples through the fifties reducing down up until final closure to steam on 3 December 1966. In that final year, this Hughes Crab from 8H Birkenhead has been bulled up for a special to the area on 27 March. *Dave Hill*

For the popular summer holidaymaker's and day tripper's trains to and from Manchester, Llandudno Junction could call upon the likes of this Royal Scot 46144 Honourable Artillery Company of Caprotti Black Five 44740 for the 1962 season as they are on their home shed displaying their 6G shed codes. *Strathwood Library Collection*

Having just been allocated here to 6G Llandudno Junction in June 1965, this double-chimneyed Standard Class 4MT previously from 6C Croes Newydd has yet to receive its new shed plate. Its next move would be to 6D Shrewsbury in August 1966. The shed buildings at Llandudno Junction would see use into the eighties as diesels continued to be stabled here. *Late Norman Browne/Strathwood Library Collection*

Bangor was another engine shed adjacent to a station affording even the youngest of spotters a chance to watch the comings and goings of everyday shed activity. A former LNWR shed it was coded 7B by the LMS and recoded to 6H by British Railways on 2 March 1952. In this view from 19 June 1949, the changes have been rung to the locomotives cab numbers and smokebox plates but loyalties to the LMS perhaps remain.
RJ Tredwell/The Transport Treasury

The extra bulling up of the smokebox door hinges suggests that Jubilee 45582 Central Provinces off of 10B Preston shed has seen recent use on something perhaps a little more prestigious than a holiday extra to here at Bangor in the mid-fifties, as it sits on the shed's 60 ft turntable. *Rail Online*

Above & opposite: Situated in a cramped site Bangor shed was not modernized by the LMS with modern coaling and ash plants, however, by 1954 the shed's roof had deteriorated badly enough for a decision to renew it completely by British Railways. This exercise saw this often busy shed shortened with the work completed during 1958. The arrival of DMUs to the area coupled with branch closures would see the allocation of steam locomotives progressively fall. But as a popular location for daytrippers and specials, the shed continued to attract both visiting steam locomotives and spotters right up to closure on 14 June 1965.

Photos: Strathwood Library Collection & The Transport Treasury

The sidings leading to the right lead to the goods yard and goods shed with Bangor's station to the left it can be seen that the footbridge above the Black Five and the Royal Scot would be attractive for young spotters in the age of steam. *Strathwood Library Collection*

The coaling and water facilities available to Bangor's shed were best described as poor, with the town's water supply sometimes being called upon to replenish water for the thirsty steam locomotives. *Strathwood Library Collection*

Holyhead with its importance to the shipping traffic across the Irish Sea and often heavily loaded trains resulted in a generous allocation of Royal Scots being based here at the start of the fifties. This first view of 7C Holyhead is from 28 March 1948 before the new nationalized railway network had begun to morph into its new identity. One of the early changes was to renew the shed roof here during 1950, followed by a change of shed code identity to 6J on 2 March 1952. This second view shows Black Fives 45116 and 44770 on 10 May 1964 along with the "hangman's gantries" erected earlier for the training of locomotive footplatemen for when they reached Crewe and the 25kv overhead wiring.

Both: Strathwood Library Collection

Pacifics at Holyhead were regulars during the fifties with Princesses, Duchess and Britannias however, the sight of Class A2 60532 Blue Peter being turned on Sunday 21 August 1966 has drawn a gathering. The 62B Dundee Tay Bridge allocated Pacific had arrived with an enthusiast's special from Manchester Central and was here for servicing prior to making the return trip. *Strathwood Library Collection*

Opposite: From a position looking down from the same over-bridge during 1965 we find this Standard Class 4MT from 5D Stoke-on-Trent being turned. The fireman has few decent sized lumps in the tender but the coal at the back looks a little more suspect for the journey back home to the potteries. Steam ended here at Holyhead shed on 5 December 1966 although diesels were to be seen using the shed for a number of years afterwards. *Strathwood Library Collection*

Left: The three-road shed at Rhyl was coded 7D before nationalization, on 2 March 1950 it adopted the code of 6K for its allocation of twenty-seven locomotives which included this ex-Lancashire & Yorkshire Railway Class 27 seen in the yard on 7 May 1955 a year before it was withdrawn. *Strathwood Library Collection*

A sub-shed to Rhyl was located here at Denbigh until it closed in September 1955. A pairing of Ivatt and Standard Class 2MTs were on shed here in March 1955. The parent shed at Rhyl closed on 11 February 1963. *Rail Online*